DATE DUE

AP *8 '97			
0017			
FE 20 '99			
MR 9 '99			
MY 6 '99			
FE 22 '00			
FE 16 '02			
JA 06 08			
MR 14			
MR 24 '10			
MY 24 '10			

DEMCO 38-297

Sojourner Truth

Sojourner Truth was born a slave in about 1797. After she was freed at the age of 30, she became a leader in the antislavery and women's rights movements.

JUNIOR · WORLD · BIOGRAPHIES

Sojourner Truth

NORMAN L. MACHT

CHELSEA JUNIORS

a division of CHELSEA HOUSE PUBLISHERS

Chelsea House Publishers
EDITOR-IN-CHIEF: Remmel Nunn
MANAGING EDITOR: Karyn Gullen Browne
COPY CHIEF: Mark Rifkin
PICTURE EDITOR: Adrian G. Allen
ART DIRECTOR: Maria Epes
ASSISTANT ART DIRECTOR: Howard Brotman
MANUFACTURING DIRECTOR: Gerald Levine
SYSTEMS MANAGER: Lindsey Ottman
PRODUCTION MANAGER: Joseph Romano
PRODUCTION COORDINATOR: Marie Claire Cebrián

JUNIOR WORLD BIOGRAPHIES

SENIOR EDITOR: Kathy Kuhtz

Staff for SOJOURNER TRUTH
EDITORIAL ASSISTANT: Danielle Janusz
PICTURE RESEARCHER: Ellen Barrett
SENIOR DESIGNER: Marjorie Zaum
COVER ILLUSTRATION: Alan Nahigian

3 5 7 9 8 6 4 2

Library of Congress Cataloging-in-Publication Data
Macht, Norman L. (Norman Lee)
  Sojourner Truth/Norman L. Macht.
    p. cm.—(Junior world biographies)
  Includes bibliographical references and index.
  Summary: A biography of the former slave who became an outspoken
antislavery and women's rights activist in the United States.
  ISBN 0-7910-1754-0
  1. Truth, Sojourner, d. 1883—Juvenile literature. 2. Afro-Americans—
Biography—Juvenile literature. 3. Abolitionists—United States—
Biography—Juvenile literature. 4. Social reformers—United States—
Biography—Juvenile literature. [1. Truth, Sojourner, d. 1883.
2. Abolitionists. 3. Reformers. 4. Afro-Americans—Biography.] I. Title.
II. Series.
E185.97.T8M34 1992   91-37268
305.5′67′092—dc20   CIP
  [B]   AC

Contents

Truth's fame as a speaker spread rapidly throughout Long Island, New York, in 1843. Her height, dignified manner, and deep voice, as well as the white shawl and bonnet she often wore, made her a memorable presence.

1

Choosing a Name

On a warm June day in 1843, a white woman working in her garden on Long Island, New York, looked up and saw an unusual sight. A very tall black woman, dressed in a long gray dress and a white turban, was walking along the road, a satchel slung over her shoulder. As the stranger came nearer, the gardener was struck by her great gloomy eyes and solemn expression.

The traveler stopped to ask for a drink of water. Her throat was parched from walking many miles, and she needed a moment's rest. The woman smiled and drew water from the well. "What is your name?" she asked. After a pause the traveler replied, "Sojourner."

It was the first time that the traveler had said the name aloud to anyone, for until that day she had gone by the name Isabella. But now, at the age of 46, she was starting a new life. That morning, she had left her housekeeping job in New York City and set out to travel the land and spread the word of God. She had decided she needed a name that would reflect her new mission, so she chose a word from the Bible that describes someone who moves from place to place. Sojourner was happy to cast off the name she had answered to while she had worn the chains of slavery.

But when the woman in the garden asked Sojourner what her last name was, she did not know what to answer, for she had no last name. She held her head high, said her name was Sojourner, and continued on her journey.

As she walked along the road, Sojourner pondered a last name. Born a slave in Upstate New York, she had had no right to a last name. Although many slaves did take the last name of their owners, Sojourner had not. She had been owned by several people before she was freed, and besides, she did not wish to use a name that belonged to a slave master.

Sojourner often talked to God and heard God's answers in her head. Now she asked God's help in choosing a proper last name. The word that came to her was *Truth*. Sojourner later said, "The Lord gave me [the name] Truth because I was to declare the truth to the people."

The story Truth had to tell was branded into her mind and body, which bore the scars of beatings with red-hot iron rods. It was not a pleasant story, but it was one people needed to hear.

In June 1843, Isabella boarded a ferry in downtown New York City and began her travels as a preacher. She had only 25 cents in her pocket, but she trusted that God would look out for her.

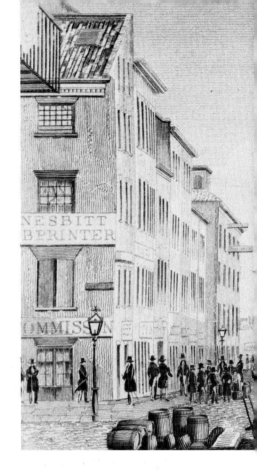

They needed to hear how her parents and brothers and sisters, as well as her own children, had suffered at the hands of cruel slave masters. Maybe if people realized how savage slavery was, they would ask their government to ban it.

Truth continued walking eastward through the farmlands of Long Island. Standing

at the edge of roadside fields, she would sing
hymns and preach to groups of white farmers,
who would pause in their work at the sound of
her deep voice. She spoke at town meetings and
church services, and she washed clothes and
scrubbed floors in exchange for food and shelter.
As the weeks went by, larger and larger crowds

came to hear the wandering preacher with the voice that rolled like thunder across the summer fields.

After a few months, Truth took a ship across Long Island Sound to Bridgeport, Connecticut, and then preached in many New England towns. When the weather turned colder, she realized she would have to find a place to stay for the winter. She was told of a *utopian community* in Massachusetts, whose members believed that everyone, including women and blacks, deserved equal rights, such as the right to vote or to own property. The community lived in a factory building and earned money by making silk cloth. Everyone shared in the work. Admiring their ideals, Sojourner decided to join them.

Some of the association members were leaders in the *abolitionist* movement, which was dedicated to bringing about the end of slavery in the United States. Truth was also introduced to people who were fighting for women's rights. (At that time, women were considered to be inferior to men. They were not allowed to vote or to work in most professions or even to speak at most public meetings.) Realizing that women were not much better off than freed slaves, Truth decided to speak out on their behalf, too.

For the rest of her life, Sojourner Truth dedicated herself to the cause of equal rights for blacks and women as well as the *civil rights* of all people. Although she could not read or write, she had a gift for the spoken word and knew the Bible by heart. With more courage than a lion tamer, she took on the white man's world, never dodged a challenge, and became the most outstanding black woman of her time, speaking out publicly against slavery and social injustice.

Isabella lived in Upstate New York until she was in her early thirties, when she traveled by boat down the Hudson River (shown here) to work in New York City.

CHAPTER

2

The Life
of a Slave

Isabella was born sometime around 1797 (her exact date of birth was not recorded) on a farm near the Hudson River in Hurley, New York. Her parents were slaves, having been captured years before by other black Africans and brought to the coast of Guinea, in West Africa. There they were sold to white slave traders who then shipped them to America.

Although slaves were not nearly as common in the northern states of the country as they were in the southern states, they were still an important part of the region's industry. For example, in Upstate New York where Isabella lived, farmers used slaves to plant and harvest their wheat, corn, tobacco, and other crops.

Like many early settlers in the Hudson River valley, Isabella's owners, the Hardenberghs, had emigrated from the Netherlands, and so they taught their slaves to speak Dutch. Isabella later learned to speak English, but she never lost her Dutch accent.

When Isabella was about 3 years old, Mr. Hardenbergh died and his son took possession of Isabella, her parents, and 10 other slaves. He moved them all into the cellar of a damp stone house he had built nearby. There was very little light and no heat in the cellar, and when it rained, water seeped in and turned the dirt floor to mud. Soon after they moved there, Isabella's brother Peter was born.

During the day, the slaves plowed and harvested their owner's fields. Isabella's parents worked especially hard and did not cause trouble for their master. To show his appreciation, he gave them a small plot of land on which they could grow their own crops. Like most slaves, Isabella and her family lived without hope for a better life. But they did have faith in God.

Sometimes at night her mother would sit under a tree with Isabella and Peter and look at the stars. "My children," she would tell them, "there is a God in the sky who hears and sees you. When you are beaten or cruelly treated, or fall into any trouble, you must ask help of Him and He will always hear and help you." Isabella never lost her faith, and her belief that she was being looked after by a powerful guardian in the sky gave her more confidence.

At night, in the dank darkness of the cellar, Isabella sometimes heard her mother crying. Once, when she asked her mother what was wrong, her mother told her, "I'm groaning to think of my poor children." Isabella learned that she had eight older brothers and sisters who were sold to other masters before she was born. It made her sad to think she would never know them.

Isabella's mother later told her the story of how her brother Michael and sister Nancy had been taken away. On a snowy winter morning, some men in a horse-drawn sleigh had stopped at the cabin. Michael was delighted when the men told him that he was going for a ride, and he

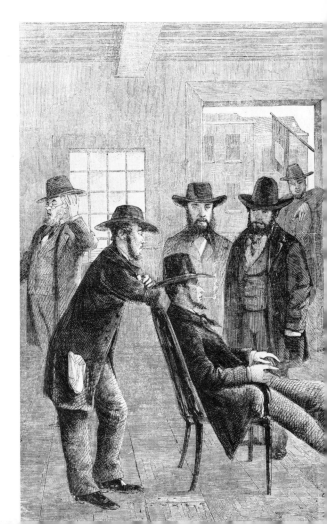

An auctioneer asks for a bid on a young black family at a slave auction in the South. Isabella and her brother were sold to new owners in 1808.

18

quickly jumped aboard. The boy became frightened, however, when he heard his sister Nancy screaming, and he turned in time to see the men put Nancy in a box on the sleigh and shut the lid tight.

Michael leapt off the sleigh and ran inside the cabin. But the men dragged him out, hoisted him up on the sleigh with them, and raced away.

Isabella's parents, who had been helpless to stop their master from selling the children to the slave traders, never saw Michael or Nancy again.

In 1808, when Isabella was about 11, a law was passed that stopped the import of slaves into the United States. But there were already more than a million of them in the country, and they could still be bought and sold. Indeed, that same year, Isabella's master died, and she and her brother were auctioned off. She was sold with a flock of sheep for $100 to a storekeeper named John Nealy, who lived in the nearby town of Kingston. Peter was sold to someone else.

Isabella's father was old and crippled and could not work, so he and Isabella's mother were freed and allowed to continue to live in the cellar. A short time later, her mother became ill and died, leaving her father to fend for himself.

The Nealys spoke only English, and Isabella knew only Dutch, so she did not understand the instructions she was given. Her owners thought she was just lazy, and they often became angry with her. One Sunday morning, John Nealy took Isabella out to the barn, tied her hands together, and beat her with hot metal rods until her back was bloody. Isabella screamed and called out to God to still her master's hand, but there was no answer.

When she told her father about her brutal beating, he persuaded a kinder man, Martin Schryver, to buy her. Her new master made his living by farming, fishing, and running a tavern at the fork of a river. Isabella was his only slave. She hoed cornfields, hauled in catches of fish, and gathered roots and herbs for the homemade beer that was sold in the tavern. By then she was nearly six feet tall and quite strong, so she was able to handle the hard work. Schryver treated her well, and by mixing with the customers in the tavern, she gradually learned to speak English. She also took up smoking a pipe, a habit she continued for many years.

Shortly after she was purchased by the tavern owner, Isabella learned that her father had

After a long day of work, slaves carry in from the fields the cotton they have harvested. Most slaves in 19th-century America worked as field hands.

starved to death. Now she was all alone in the world, with no idea where the rest of her family might be.

Isabella was an industrious worker and her master valued her, but when he was offered the chance to make a profit by selling her, he was unable to refuse. So at the age of 13, she was taken from the quiet life she had been leading to a nearby farm, where she would be among 10 other slaves and 2 white maids. They were all under the thumb of a mistress who was as mean as a wicked stepmother in a fairy tale. No matter how hard she worked in the fields and in the kitchen, Isabella could not please her mistress, Mrs. Dumont. But Isabella's mother had taught her to be a polite and hard worker, so she continued to do more than any of the other slaves.

In 1814, Mr. Dumont matched Isabella with one of his older slaves, a man named Thomas. During the next 12 years, she and Thomas had 5 children: Diana, Elizabeth, Hannah, Peter, and Sophie. Isabella loved her children very much, but caring for them was difficult at times. When she worked in the fields, she would put her infant in a basket, tie a rope to each handle, and suspend the basket from a tree branch. Then one of her older children would push it like a swing to keep the baby quiet.

Year after year, Isabella planted corn, chopped wood, hauled buckets of water, and raised her children. She never stopped talking to God, asking again and again for only one thing: freedom.

The cabins in which slaves lived were often drafty, windowless buildings. Like Isabella's mother, many slaves became ill and died as a result of the cold, damp quarters.

3

Escape to Freedom

Isabella's hope of being freed was not just a day-dream to make her life more bearable. She knew that not all blacks were slaves and that most of the states in the North and the Midwest did not allow people to own slaves. In these free states, as they were called, lived many former slaves who had run away from their masters or bought their freedom by giving them all the money they had earned doing extra work.

Some of the former slaves were working toward freedom for all their people. For example, around the year 1800, free blacks in Philadelphia, Pennsylvania, had asked Congress to gradually end all slavery. They were turned down by a vote of 85 to 1, but the petition, or written request, nevertheless called attention to the antislavery cause.

In addition, not all whites supported slavery. From the time the first slaves were brought to the American colonies, there were individuals who believed that it was wrong for one human being to own another. The *Quakers*, a religious group known for their deep faith, opposition to war, and plain style of dress, worked especially hard to thwart slavery. And in the early 1800s, more and more whites were joining the antislavery movement.

In 1824, Isabella's dream of being free suddenly seemed more promising. She learned that the New York State government, under pressure from the abolitionists, had passed a law that would free all slaves who were at least 28 years old as of July 4, 1827. Male slaves who were younger were to become free when they turned 28, and female slaves would be free at age 25.

Because no one knew for sure when Isabella had been born, the Dumonts agreed she would be eligible to be freed in 1827. Isabella thanked God that her Freedom Day was only three years away. When her master then promised to free her a year earlier if she worked extra hard, she believed all her prayers had been answered. But the next year she cut her hand so badly on a harvesting tool that she could not work as fast, and when her promised Freedom Day came, Mr. Dumont would not let her go.

Isabella was furious at her master for breaking his promise, and decided to run away. She wished she could take her children with her, but she knew she would not get very far with five children in tow. She would have to leave them behind. She stayed to finish spinning the year's harvest of wool because she was afraid her children might be mistreated if she did not complete the job.

When she was finally ready to leave one night in early October, she quietly made a bundle of clothes and food while the other slaves slept. She planned to leave a few hours before daylight so she would be miles away by the time the sun came up. At the last minute, she decided to take her youngest child, Sophie, with her. She knew that the other slaves would look after her older children. As she walked silently out of the house, the sun was just beginning to light up the sky.

Not until the sun was high did she dare stop to rest. Then she faced another problem: where to go. As if guided by an unseen hand, she reached the home of a farmer she knew. He directed her to the house of a Quaker couple named Van Wagener. The Van Wageners listened to her story and offered Isabella a home and a job as a freedwoman, not as a slave. Isabella later recalled:

> After they gave me supper, they took me into a room where there was a great, tall white bed, and they told me to sleep there. Well, honey, I was

kind of scared when they left me alone with that great white bed, 'cause I never had been in a bed in my life. It never came into my mind they could mean me to sleep in it. So I just camped down under it on the floor. . . . In the morning when they came in, they asked me if I hadn't been asleep, and I said, 'Yes, I never slept better.' And they said, 'Why, you haven't been in the bed.' And says I, 'Laws, you didn't think of such a thing as my sleeping in that there bed, did you?'

Mr. Dumont soon tracked down Isabella at the Van Wagener house and demanded that she return to his farm. Isabella refused. Van Wagener stepped in and offered Dumont money if he would give up his claim. The two men agreed to a sum, and Isabella was free at last. But she was saddened when she learned that Dumont had sold her son, Peter, to a man who had then sent the boy to a plantation in Alabama, a state in which there was no Freedom Day on the calendar. Isabella begged the Dumonts and the people who had bought

An illustration from the antislavery newspaper Emancipator *shows a slave being separated from her child. Isabella experienced similar anguish when she learned that her son had been sold to a new owner in the South.*

Peter to bring him back, but they all ignored her pleas.

Fortunately, some of the Van Wageners' friends told Isabella that there was a law against sending slaves out of the state and that she could sue to get her son back. So Isabella went from house to house along the dusty roads, asking for donations to cover the cost of hiring a lawyer.

She managed to collect enough money, and the lawyer she hired arranged to have Peter brought back for a court hearing.

The court hearing was finally scheduled in the spring of 1828. But when they went before the judge, Peter claimed that Isabella was not his mother and begged his master not to make him go with her. The judge suspected that the young boy had been forced to say these things and ordered that Peter go with his mother. Outside the courtroom, Peter told Isabella he had been threatened with a beating if he told the truth.

At that time, it was remarkable for a black woman to file a lawsuit and win a court case against a white man. But Isabella did not care much about that. She was happy just to be reunited with her son. She was horrified, though, when she saw that Peter's body was covered with scars from many whippings. The mistreatment had scarred his mind, too, and Isabella knew it would not be easy to teach him to have faith in people again.

Isabella had a comfortable room and enough to eat at the Van Wageners' house, and they were kind to her. But, having been with them two years, she felt it was time to move on. She was anxious to earn money so that she could buy her own house someday.

Talking to other servants in the town, Isabella learned that high wages could be made working for wealthy merchants in New York City. After thinking about it for a while, Isabella decided to move there. Although she would miss her children, she knew she had to earn a living.

Toward the end of the summer of 1828, Isabella brought little Sophie to the Dumont farm to live with her older daughters. In New York City, there would be no one to take care of Sophie while Isabella was at work. Then she and Peter said farewell to the others and sailed down the Hudson River to New York on a big riverboat. Peter loved being aboard the ship.

The big city excited Isabella. Having spent so many years on farms and in little villages, she was in awe of the city's bustle of activity, its wide cobblestone streets, and its tall buildings. But she and Peter were shocked to see how many poor people crowded into the *slums*.

There were many freed slaves in the city, and more were pouring in every day. Their life was hard. They had virtually no education, and almost no schools were open to them. Those who had a trade or some skills found that white workers often refused to work alongside them. Also, on the streets of the city roamed slave catchers, men who made money kidnapping runaway and freed slaves and selling them back into bondage in the South.

With the help of a white schoolteacher, Isabella soon found well-paying work as a servant in the homes of several wealthy families, and Peter attended a school that trained seamen. Unfortunately, he fell in with a gang of troublemakers and began skipping school and hanging out on the streets. Isabella pleaded with Peter to be good, but he did not change his ways.

Isabella took comfort in talking to God. But she could not find a church in the city that allowed blacks to attend Sunday services with whites. The churches either held separate services for blacks, made them sit apart from whites, or barred them from the church altogether. Isabella refused to accept these unfair rules, so she became a member of a small all-black church.

She soon joined a group that walked through the city streets singing hymns to the poor. Singing was something Isabella had done since she was a little girl. She and the other slaves had often sung while they worked in the fields. It helped them survive their difficult life. The songs they made up were often about rising up against the master and being free. The overseers in the fields did not detect the songs' rebellious meanings because the slaves hid the message in poetic language.

But as much as Isabella liked to sing to the city's poor people, it did not seem to be doing enough for them. So she devoted her free time to working at a shelter for homeless young women, teaching them how to cook, sew, and clean house so that they could find work as household servants.

The director of the shelter for young women was a preacher named Elijah Pierson. Isabella was impressed with the seemingly saintlike Pierson, and when he and another self-proclaimed prophet started a religious community in 1832, Isabella decided to join them. Known as the Kingdom, the community was located on a farm, 30 miles north of the city, that was owned by a couple named Benjamin and Ann Folger. Isabella and

An 1849 view of New York City. Isabella was excited by the city's bustle of activity but was shocked to see how many poor people were crowded into its slums.

the Folgers gave their life savings to the so-called prophets, who spent more time performing strange religious rituals and spending other people's money than doing any good deeds.

After two years, Isabella returned to New York City. She was fed up with the Kingdom and wanted to be near her son, who had fallen into more trouble. Soon after she returned, she learned that one of the prophets had died and that his relatives had accused the other prophet of poisoning him and stealing his money. Isabella got caught up in the scandal. One New York City newspaper printed a story about the Kingdom based on Mr. Folger's comments, claiming that Isabella was an evil witch who had brought about the destruction of the Kingdom.

A reporter from another newspaper gave Isabella a chance to tell her side of the story and he encouraged her to sue the first newspaper for *slander*, or unfair reporting. Isabella followed his advice and won a $125 judgment.

For the next several years, Isabella worked

for a family named Whiting. Isabella's biggest challenge during this period was trying to help Peter straighten out his life. He had been expelled from school and arrested for *vandalism* several times as well. In desperation, she asked the advice of a black barber who was known in the city for helping black youths stay out of trouble. He suggested that because Peter loved ships so much, he ought to join the crew of a whaling ship.

In 1839, Peter sailed from New York City aboard a whaling ship bound for the South Pacific. About a year later, Isabella received a letter from him. He called the ship "unlucky" and expressed to Isabella how sorry he was for all the worry he had caused her.

Isabella received two more letters from Peter during the next year, but after that, she heard nothing. She was worried the ship had sunk in a storm at sea. She kept hoping another letter would arrive, but she never heard from Peter again. For the rest of her life, she carried her son's letters around with her.

An advertisement warns blacks in Boston, Massachusetts, to be on the lookout for slave catchers hunting for fugitives in the area.

By 1843, Isabella was tired of New York City. It had offered her nothing but hard work and suffering. She continued to save her money so she could buy a house, although she realized that it was too late to reunite her family as she had once planned. Peter was gone, and her older daughters, freed from the Dumont farm, had each married and would soon begin to raise families of their own.

As Isabella began to dream about starting a new life away from New York City, she realized she wanted to share with others her experiences as a slave, a mother, and a Christian. The joys and sorrows of her life had given her wisdom about human kindness and cruelty. She talked to God every day, and she was certain that God wanted her to travel the land and help the oppressed.

So one day in the summer of 1843, Isabella tucked a few dresses in a pillowcase, said farewell to the Whitings, and—with only 25 cents in her pocket—set out on her journey.

To raise money for her travels, Sojourner Truth sold
postcards with her photograph and her personal
motto printed on them.

I Sell the Shadow to Support the Substance.

SOJOURNER TRUTH.

4

Turning the World Right Side Up

Isabella took a ferry from downtown New York City to Brooklyn. From there she walked to Long Island, where she spent the summer preaching to potato farmers and tending to the sick in exchange for food and shelter. At the age of 46, she finally felt truly free. To celebrate this turning point, she changed her name to Sojourner Truth, and it was by this name that her fame spread through the towns of Long Island and beyond.

Although she did not have a particular direction in mind, her purpose was clear, and it drew her north to New England, which was the center of the abolitionist movement. She eventually arrived in Massachusetts and joined a utopian community called the Northampton Association of Education and Industry. Truth never thought twice about speaking her mind at the association's meetings, and she quickly earned the respect of the other members.

Truth met many important public leaders through the association. William Lloyd Garrison, a well-known abolitionist, visited the community often. He had started an antislavery newspaper and had founded two influential antislavery societies. The societies published pamphlets and held meetings to persuade people that slavery was wrong and should be stopped.

Truth also met Frederick Douglass, an escaped slave who had taught himself to read and write and who had become a powerful speaker. Unlike Truth, Douglass had turned away from

Frederick Douglass, an escaped slave who became a leader in the abolitionist movement, encouraged Truth to keep up her fight against slavery.

religion. He did not trust the preachers in their big churches who spoke of love and equality but then shrank from denouncing slavery. Douglass broadened Truth's understanding of white people's *prejudice* toward blacks—their judgment that blacks are inferior just because their skin is a different color. He and the other leaders Truth met inspired her to keep fighting what she considered to be the white man's greatest sin: the enslavement of her people. (The sin of slavery, however, was not limited to whites. In 1830, a U.S. *census* reported that 3,777 black families, most of whom lived in the South, owned slaves themselves.)

The abolitionists taught Truth the power of the printed and spoken word, although handing out pamphlets, selling newspapers, and giving speeches, she learned, were not their only methods. Many of those who opposed slavery, both whites and blacks, were putting their very life at risk to further the cause of equality.

One such individual was Prudence Crandall, a white teacher who in 1833 opened the first all-black school for girls, in Canterbury, Connecticut, and was thrown in jail for doing so. That same year, Oberlin College in Ohio had opened its doors as an *integrated* college, despite the threats of those who violently opposed whites and blacks attending the same institution.

In addition, since the beginning of the 19th century, northern free blacks as well as white abolitionists had been running the Underground Railroad, a network of people all over the nation who hid runaway slaves in their houses and barns or guided them to the free states and Canada.

Although the antislavery movement was gradually gaining power in the 1840s, the Northampton Association was having trouble making ends meet, and in 1846, it was forced to break up. Truth then went to work in the home of George Benson, one of the abolitionist organizers. Shortly thereafter, her friend Olive Gilbert offered to write Truth's *memoirs*. Frederick Douglass had published his memoirs the year before, and like other slave memoirs, they had become a best-seller. Gilbert felt the story of Truth's early life as a slave would encourage more northerners to turn against slavery.

The Narrative of Sojourner Truth: A Northern Slave was printed and ready to be sold in 1850. But none of the bookstores would take it. The disagreement between people who were proslavery and those who were antislavery had become bitter; violent clashes between the two groups were occurring throughout the nation, especially in the South. No bookstore owners wanted to carry the book and risk having their windows smashed or their building burned down by proslavery mobs.

Truth was disappointed when Gilbert told her the news, but she would not be defeated. She resolved to sell the book herself. In the years that followed, she brought along copies of her book to all the public meetings she attended and sold many hundreds of them. In later years, she also sold copies of songs she had written as well as postcards with her photograph on them.

Truth joined another battle for freedom: the women's rights campaign. For several years, she had heard people lecture about the unfair treatment of women; now she was ready to speak out about the issue herself.

Like the antislavery movement, the women's rights movement relied on oratory, or public speaking, to persuade more people to join the cause. Organizers would often rent a public hall or a meetinghouse and put up posters announcing a lecture on women's rights. People would come in wagons and on foot from all over the countryside to listen to the spellbinding speakers. (There was no radio or television back then, so attending lectures of all kinds was the chief form of entertainment.)

The speakers at abolitionist gatherings—and even at many women's rights meetings—were almost always men. It was not considered proper for a woman to speak at a public meeting. So when Truth would stand up to speak, there would be a commotion in the audience. There she was, not only a woman—but a black woman.

Truth also surprised her audiences with her speaking style. Most orators strove to pronounce their words beautifully, and they often used formal, flowery language. Sojourner Truth did not. Instead, she cast her spell with the rough, uneducated manner and language of an unschooled slave girl who never learned to read or write. Unlike some orators who droned on for hours, Truth impressed her listeners with her ability to get to the heart of complex issues in a few words.

One time, at a meeting in Boston, Frederick Douglass declared to the crowd that slavery could be ended only by bloodshed. Without hesitating, Truth called out sharply, "Frederick, is God dead?" Douglass later described Truth as:

[She is] that strange compound of wit and wisdom, of wild enthusiasm, and flint-like common sense, who seemed to feel it her duty to trip me up in my speeches and to ridicule my efforts to speak and act like a person of cultivation and refinement.

Douglass was not the only one who got a taste of Truth's bold comments. In 1850, she attended a convention on women's rights in Worcester, Massachusetts. After listening to several lengthy speeches by educated and distinguished individuals, she grew impatient and declared: "Sisters, I ain't clear what you'd be after. If women want any rights more than they's got, why don't they just take them, and not be talking about it?"

And at a convention in Akron, Ohio, in 1852, Truth sat for two days listening as ministers and other men spelled out how women were weaker and less intelligent than men and therefore should not be allowed to vote. One man went so far as to say that God intended for men to have more power than women because he made Christ a man.

Truth could not believe the women in the audience were allowing the men to make such outrageous statements. Looking around her, she saw that not one woman had dared to stand up and object to the speaker's comments. Truth rose from her chair. Although she could hear the gasps of shock in the audience and shouts of, "No! Don't let her speak!" she was unafraid and walked slowly up the steps of the stage.

Drawing herself erect so she looked even taller than her six feet, she pointed to the man who had claimed that women were weaker than men and boomed: "Ain't I a woman?" She rolled the sleeves of her dress up to show muscular, skinny arms. "I have plowed, and planted, and worked as hard as any man, and eat as much, too. And ain't I a woman? My mother bore ten children and saw them sold off to slavery, and when I cried with my mother's grief, nobody but Jesus heard me! And ain't I a woman?"

Taking on the question of God's intentions, she said, "And whar did your Christ come from?" A witness at the meeting later said, "Rolling thunder couldn't have stilled the crowd, as did those deep wonderful tones, as she stood there with outstretched arms and eyes of fire. Raising her voice still louder, she repeated, 'Whar did your Christ come from? From God and a woman. Man had nothin' to do wid Him.' "

Truth raised her hand to quiet the applause and then called on the women in the audience to turn the world "right side up again."

That same year, a white writer from New England named Harriet Beecher Stowe published a novel entitled *Uncle Tom's Cabin*. It brought the evils of slavery to the attention of people all over the nation and helped persuade many of them to fight against slavery. But the book also added to the tensions between the northern abolitionists and those southerners who supported slavery.

As the controversy about slavery worsened, abolitionist meetings erupted in violence more often. During the mid-1850s, Truth traveled

Harriet Beecher Stowe's popular novel Uncle Tom's Cabin *brought the evils of slavery to the attention of people all over the nation.*

throughout the Midwest, giving speeches on behalf of the abolitionist cause, and she often had to put up with people in the crowd shouting rude words at her. She used her sense of humor to silence them. Sometimes, however, stones were hurled in her direction or she was threatened with clubs.

Much of this hostility stemmed from a law that Congress had approved a few years earlier, in 1850. Called the Fugitive Slave Act, it was created to calm the South, which had threatened to leave the *Union* and set up its own government if slavery was outlawed. The act declared that slaves were property and that "all good citizens" in the free states must turn in runaway slaves to the law so that they could be sent back to their masters. It was so unjust that many people in the North became active abolitionists.

On October 29, 1864, Truth visited President Abraham Lincoln in his office at the White House and thanked him for all he had done on behalf of blacks. This painting shows the president examining her "Book of Life."

5

Visiting
President
Lincoln

As more territories in the West were admitted to the Union, the issue of slavery became even more hotly debated. All across America, people argued about whether the new states should be free states or slave states. In 1854, Congress passed a bill that would push the country toward war. Called the Kansas-Nebraska Act, the bill made Kansas and Nebraska U.S. territories and declared that the people living in these regions should decide for themselves whether they wanted slavery. This touched off open warfare as the pro- and antislavery forces fought for power in these new territories.

In 1857, Sojourner Truth decided to settle down for a while. She was 60 years old, and she was tired. She found a place to live in Battle Creek, Michigan, a town she had visited on her speaking tours, and began to make many friends. Later that year, however, the abolitionists desperately needed her help. The Supreme Court had just handed down the Dred Scott decision, which held that Congress had no authority to pass laws restricting slavery in any of the states. This ruling was a major blow to the antislavery cause, for it opened the door for the spread of slavery into the new states being formed in the West.

So Truth put on her traveling shoes, packed her bags, and hit the speaking trail. She went from one midwestern town to another, giving speeches wherever she could attract a crowd. Newspapers reported her appearances; she was ridiculed by some, praised by others. Everywhere she went, she heard talk about war. As much as Truth wanted to see the end of slavery, she still hoped it could be abolished without bloodshed.

In 1860, Sojourner's daughter Elizabeth moved to Battle Creek with her two children. A little later, her daughter Diana joined them. Having her family reunited at last gave Truth great comfort, and she returned home often to be with them and to earn money by doing housework.

Later that year, Abraham Lincoln was elected president. Five months later, in April 1861, the feud between the North and the South burst wide open—the Civil War began. Sojourner Truth went on the road, rallying support for the Union's war effort. The mood of the country was even uglier now. Indiana, fearing that swarms of escaped or freed slaves would come into the state, passed a law forbidding any blacks to cross its borders. But it could not stop Truth. In the fall of 1862, she traveled boldly through Indiana delivering her speeches. Whenever she was arrested, her supporters rallied around and got her out of

Abraham Lincoln (in top hat) meets with officers who commanded the Union troops at the Battle of Antietam, in September 1862.

jail. In one Indiana town, a proslavery mob threatened to burn down the lecture hall where she was scheduled to speak. Truth told them, "Then I will speak upon the ashes."

In spite of the energy she showed during her speechmaking, Truth was worn out from her travels and from her work cooking and cleaning in Battle Creek. In the winter of 1862, she became very ill. Rumors spread throughout the nation that she was dying. Word of her illness reached the abolitionist newspaper *Anti-Slavery Standard*,

and its editors collected donations for her. She used the money to buy a house in Battle Creek.

Truth's spirits were lifted when President Lincoln signed the *Emancipation Proclamation*, which declared that all slaves in the South would be set free as of January 1, 1863. One day in 1864, Truth took it into her head to go to Washington, D.C., to see President Lincoln. She wanted to assure Lincoln that the country was behind him and that he would be reelected in November. Setting out with one of her grandsons, the 67-year-old Truth traveled to the nation's capital, stopping in several towns along the way to give speeches.

On the morning of October 29, 1864, Truth waited in the White House reception room for her appointment to see the president. When she was ushered into Lincoln's office and had settled in a chair, she said, "I never heard of you before you were put in for president." Lincoln laughed and replied, "I heard of you years and years before I ever thought of being president."

Truth then thanked the president for all he had done for black Americans and told him she was confident he would be reelected. Lincoln in turn thanked her for her encouragement and then signed her "Book of Life," a notebook full of autographs of people she had met over the years. He wrote, "For Aunty Sojourner Truth, A. Lincoln, Oct. 29, 1864."

That November, as Truth had predicted, Lincoln was reelected. By then, she had decided to stay in Washington for a while. The city was overflowing with freed slaves who had made their way north to the nation's capital because it was where their hero, Abraham Lincoln, lived. They needed Truth's help. They were hungry, homeless, and without the skills that would enable them to get jobs.

Hundreds of black families crowded into *refugee* camps called freedmen's villages. These areas were jammed with windowless shacks and tents—all without heat or plumbing. Because of these conditions, sickness and disease spread rapidly through the camps, claiming many lives.

Blacks were also in constant danger of being kidnapped by slave traders, who would smuggle them back to bondage. The slave traders threatened to kill anyone who gave information about the slave trade to federal *marshals*.

Washington hospitals were filled with wounded soldiers whose need for medicine, nursing, and food taxed the city's resources even more. Truth worked as a nurse and visited the refugee camps, reminding the former slaves that the law

After Union armies liberated large sections of the
South, thousands of freed slaves began to move north
and settle in refugee camps around Washington, D.C.

was on their side and that they should use it against the slave traders. Policemen who had been bribed by the slave traders tried to stop Truth from assisting the blacks in the camps. They told her that they would arrest her if she continued to stir up trouble. She boldly replied, "If you put me in the guard house, I will make the United States rock like a cradle." Her work gave her a renewed sense of purpose, and she began to feel stronger than she had in some time.

Truth was in Washington on the night of April 14, 1865, when President Lincoln was shot while watching a play at Ford's Theater. He died the following morning. Lincoln's death devastated Truth; she knew that her people had lost a great friend.

In this artist's drawing, a black man casts his vote into the ballot box. Although blacks were given the right to vote after the Civil War, many whites kept them from voting by terrorizing them with threats of physical violence.

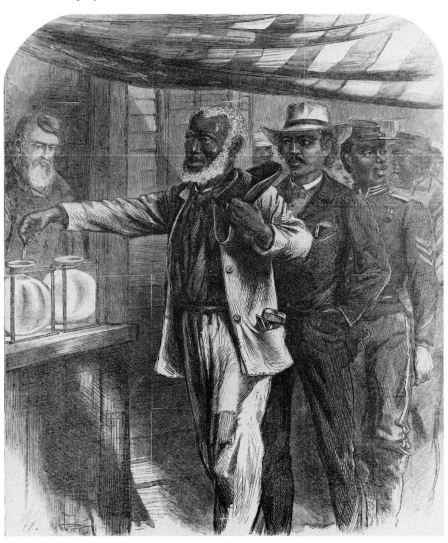

6

The Unfinished Work

In 1865, a month after Lincoln's death, the last of the South's armies surrendered to Union forces. The Civil War was over. It had lasted four years and had claimed hundreds of thousands of lives. Although the cost was high, the battle against slavery had been won.

Later that year, Truth rejoiced with millions of others when Congress passed the Thirteenth Amendment to the Constitution, which outlawed slavery throughout the land. But freedom, Truth had come to realize, is not the same as justice. In Washington, she came up against prejudice every day. When she tried to take a horse-drawn streetcar to work, she was told she could not ride in the same streetcar as the whites. Truth refused to obey the law, and one day she marched into the office of the streetcar company president and filed a complaint. Shortly thereafter, *segregated* streetcars were abolished. The rules, however, were not always obeyed. Some drivers still refused to stop for blacks. One day when a streetcar conductor rode right by Truth without stopping, she was so angry she stepped in front of the next car that came along, shouting, "I want to ride! I want to ride!" The streetcar was forced to stop, and she jumped on and sat down in a front seat.

A few years later, the U.S. government took a step to curb such *discrimination* and to improve the life of blacks by passing the Fifteenth Amendment to the Constitution. It guaranteed the right to vote to all citizens, regardless of "race, color or previous condition of servitude." Freed slaves now had the right to vote in every state. (However, the amendment said nothing about allowing women to vote.)

But the Fifteenth Amendment did not stop state governments from coming up with ways to keep blacks from voting. They charged fees that most blacks could not afford or required black voters to pass a written test that not even a highly educated person could pass. Nor did it prevent whites from threatening black men. For example, many white employers warned their black workers that they would be fired if they registered to vote; white landlords warned their black tenants that they would be kicked out of their housing. Some whites even threatened to break the leg of any black man who tried to vote or failed to vote as he was told.

In 1868, distressed by the racial hatred she saw, Truth and her grandson traveled through the East and the Midwest. She gave speeches and asked people to sign a petition that demanded the U.S. government give land in the West to the former slaves so that they could have a fair chance at a decent life. She believed this plan would be a good way for the government to pay them back for all the work they had done as slaves toward building the nation. Despite the power of Truth's speechmaking, it would take four years to collect enough signatures to give the idea some force, and the request was never granted.

The government's promises to improve life for blacks were broken again and again in the years that followed. In the 1870s, *white supremacists* came to power in the South. They formed groups such as the *Ku Klux Klan*, which kidnapped and murdered blacks without fear of punishment. They passed laws to keep blacks from advancing. Conditions for blacks were almost as bad as they had been under slavery. Blacks were free, but they had no power, no voice, no schools, no training, and no land. What little legal and economic status they had gained after the Civil

War was rapidly being taken away. They could work only in the fields or in menial jobs. This work was the same as they had done as slaves, but now they had to feed themselves and find their own housing. They often ended up in rickety dirt-floored houses that were as bleak as the cabins and cellars they had called home as slaves.

Nevertheless, there was some progress. In 1875, Congress passed a civil rights bill prohibiting discrimination in public buildings. A black from Mississippi, Blanche K. Bruce, served a full term in the U.S. Senate. Other blacks from the South were elected to Congress and helped pass laws that allowed black children to attend free schools in the South. In 1881, Booker T. Washington opened Tuskegee Institute with a $2,000 grant from the Alabama legislature to give blacks an opportunity for advanced education.

But these individuals, Truth knew, were the exceptions. For most blacks, freedom could not be translated into equality and dignity. More and more, she saw that the battle for black freedom had only just begun. Now in her eighties, she was too old and ill to continue the fight.

One morning in early November 1883, Olive Gilbert visited Truth at her home in Battle Creek and found her in extreme pain. Yet when Truth saw her old friend, she smiled, and with a faraway look in her eyes, she began to sing her favorite hymn, one that she often used to gather crowds for her speeches. She sang: "It was early in the morning / It was early in the morning / Just at the break of day / When He rose, when He rose, when He rose / And went to heaven on a cloud."

Two weeks later, on November 26, Sojourner Truth died. Her daughters Elizabeth and Diana were at her side. She was 86 years old. Two days later, nearly a thousand people crowded inside and around the little church near her house for what was said to be the biggest funeral ever seen in Battle Creek.

Sojourner Truth helped make possible the day when her fellow slaves would shake loose

Truth's daughter Diana Corbin (shown here) was among those who cared for her during her final years in Battle Creek, Michigan.

their chains and be free, and her rousing speeches helped convince women that they, too, were trapped in a kind of bondage. But ultimately, it was not only blacks and women she championed. For whenever she raised her deep, magical voice before a crowd, Sojourner Truth stood for something larger: the dignity and equality of all humankind.

Further Reading

Other Biographies of Sojourner Truth

Claflin, Edward Beecher. *Sojourner Truth and the Struggle for Freedom.* New York: Barron's, 1987.

Ferris, Jeri. *Walking the Road to Freedom: A Story About Sojourner Truth.* Minneapolis: Carolrhoda, 1988.

Related Books

Lester, Julius. *To Be a Slave.* New York: Dial Press, 1968.

Levinson, Nancy Smiler. *The First Women Who Spoke Out.* Minneapolis: Dillon, 1983.

McKissack, Patricia, and Frederick McKissack. *Frederick Douglass: The Black Lion.* Chicago: Childrens Press, 1987.

Scott, John A. *A Woman Against Slavery: The Story of Harriet Beecher Stowe.* New York: HarperCollins, 1978.

Glossary

abolitionist   a person who supported the movement to abolish, or end, the practice of slavery in the United States

census   an official count of the people living in a country or district

civil rights   the personal and property rights recognized by a government and guaranteed by a constitution and its laws

discrimination   the unfair treatment of an individual, group, or race

integrated   open to people of all races

Ku Klux Klan   a secret, all-white society whose members believe in the superiority of the white race

marshals   Federal officers who enforce the law and perform duties similar to those of a sheriff

memoirs   a person's written record of personal life experiences

prejudice   a feeling or opinion, usually negative, that has been formed about something or someone before all the facts are known

Quakers   members of the Society of Friends, a religious group that was established in 17th-century England and that believes that no priest or ritual is needed to communicate with God; Quakers believe in the equality of all men and women, and they oppose war

refugee   a person who escapes from a dangerous place to an area that seems to offer shelter and protection

segregated   restricted to members of one group or one race

slander   a false statement that harms a person's reputation

slums   run-down, overcrowded areas of a city, where poor people live

Union   the United States of America, especially during the Civil War

utopian community   a group that lives according to its members' ideas for a perfect society

vandalism   the deliberate damaging or destroying of property

white supremacists   people who believe that whites are superior to blacks and that blacks should be ruled by whites

Chronology

ca. 1797	Isabella, later known as Sojourner Truth, is born in Hurley, New York.
1800	Isabella's owner, Mr. Hardenbergh, dies; his son Charles becomes Isabella's master.
1808	Charles Hardenbergh dies; Isabella is sold to John Nealy, and her mother dies shortly thereafter.
1809	Isabella's father persuades Martin Schryver to buy her; Isabella's father dies.
1810	Martin Schryver sells Isabella to John Dumont.
1814	Mr. Dumont matches Isabella with Thomas, another slave, with whom she will have five children.
1826–27	Isabella escapes to the home of the Van Wageners, who purchase her freedom from Mr. Dumont.
1828	Isabella goes to court and succeeds in getting back her son Peter; she and Peter move to New York City.

1832	Isabella joins a religious community called the Kingdom.
1834	Isabella leaves the Kingdom to return to New York City.
1843	Isabella leaves New York City to become a traveling preacher; she changes her name to Sojourner Truth.
1850	*The Narrative of Sojourner Truth: A Northern Slave* is published.
1857	Truth moves to Battle Creek, Michigan; she travels throughout the Midwest, speaking on behalf of the abolitionist cause.
1861–62	Truth travels through the Midwest to rally support for the Union.
1864	Truth meets President Abraham Lincoln.
1868	Truth travels through the East and the Midwest with a petition asking the U.S. government to give land in the West to former slaves.
Nov. 26, 1883	Sojourner Truth dies in Battle Creek, Michigan.

Index

Norman L. Macht holds a bachelor of philosophy degree from the University of Chicago and a master's degree in political science from Sonoma State University. He writes extensively on finance and sports history and has written several biographies for the Chelsea House BASEBALL LEGENDS series. Macht is also the author of *Christopher Columbus* in the Chelsea House JUNIOR WORLD BIOGRAPHIES series. He is currently writing a biography on the American sportsman Connie Mack and is founder and president of a features syndicate based in Newark, Delaware.

Picture Credits